Trinidad and Tobago:
A souvenir in pictures

Introduction

Trinidad and Tobago lies at the southern end of the Caribbean island chain, close to the Venezuelan coast. The two islands were joined together as a single state at the end of the last century, and make a neat, contrasting pair. Trinidad is the industrial and commercial centre, where life goes on at a faster pace; while Tobago has the classic white-sand beaches, the coral reefs, the holiday mood, a more relaxed tempo. It is only a twelve-minute flight between the two islands on the busy DC-9s of BWIA International, the national airline.

The islands were first settled by Amerindians, pushing northwards from South America. In time, Trinidad became a Spanish colony, an outpost in the fruitless Spanish quest for El Dorado, the city of gold; it was snatched by a British fleet in 1797 and remained British until independence in 1962. Its people are descended from the Spanish, French and English settlers, from the Africans who were brought to Trinidad to work the sugar plantations and the Indians who succeeded them after emancipation, and from people who came from China, from the Middle East and the Mediterranean. Tobago, on the other hand, was fought over for decades by the British and the French, pirates and buccaneers, even colonists from Latvia, before it became a British colony in the late eighteenth century and was joined onto Trinidad at the end of the nineteenth century.

This is the country which has given the world calypso, the revolutionary music of the steel orchestras, writers like V S and Shiva Naipaul, musicians like Winifred Atwell, the Angostura Bitters which are found in every self-respecting bar and kitchen in the world — and one of the world's great spectacles and experiences, the exuberant pre-Lenten Carnival.

But there is much more still. The quiet, cool forests of the northern range. The Atlantic surf pounding the empty, coconut-palmed beaches of Manzanilla. The silent underwater world of Buccoo Reef. The infectious Spanish rhythms of parang, the music of Christmas. More species of birds and butterflies than are found anywhere else in the Caribbean. First-rate golf. The flavour of a good Indian *roti*. . . But perhaps the pictures can say it best.

Port of Spain

Amerindians were the first people to settle this part of Trinidad's coast, beside the Gulf of Paria, with the mountains of Venezuela on the horizon. The Spanish made their capital here in the 1750s. Now a city of 350,000 people, Port of Spain is Trinidad and Tobago's commercial and administrative heart.

Rebuilt in 1904, the Red House is the seat of Parliament, whose two houses meet in the north wing (right).

In the heart of downtown Port of Spain is Woodford Square, laid out more than 160 years ago beside the Anglican Cathedral of the Holy Trinity (in the background). The scene of many a big political rally, this is where Trinidad and Tobago's first Prime Minister, Dr Eric Williams, drew the crowds and promised them a 'University of Woodford Square'.

Queen's Royal College, beside the Queen's Park Savannah, dates back to 1904. Novelist V S Naipaul and Dr Eric Williams went to school here.

Whitehall, overlooking the Savannah, for many years the office of the Prime Minister.

The ornate houses lining the western side of the Savannah, including Queen's Royal College and Whitehall, have been nicknamed 'The Magnificent Seven'. Stollmeyer's Castle, at the northern end, was built by a family from Germany and conjures up visions of Scottish baronial castles.

The President's House is on the north side of the Savannah, next to the Botanic Gardens.

Ornate 'gingerbread' craftwork was typical of many city houses, as in this one by the Savannah.

The Queen's Park Savannah is the lungs of Port of Spain, home of joggers, cricketers, coconut vendors, horse-racing and much else.

Cricket is a game played and followed with devotion, and the Queen's Park Oval, with its backdrop of hills, is one of the most beautiful cricket grounds in the world.

Sea Lots is the home for many fishing and trading vessels.

The twin towers of the
Financial Complex house the
Central Bank, the Finance
Ministry and the Prime
Minister's office.

The National Stadium outside
Port of Spain handles athletic
and other sports meetings at
the highest level.

Trinidad

Trinidad's steep, rugged north coast conceals dozens of secluded beaches.

High in the hills of the northern range, monks of the Benedictine order built their monastery, Mount St Benedict. From there, the broad central plain stretches away to the horizon, and the forested hills lead towards the Atlantic coast in the east.

Soft evening light filters through the palms at the mile-long Las Cuevas beach ('the caves') on the north coast.

Thick forest covers much of the northern range, making these lovely hills a rich habitat for birds and butterflies and Trinidad's wild animals.

High in the hills of the northern range, on the road from Arima to Blanchisseuse, lies the Asa Wright Nature Centre, a superb centre for studying the rich variety of bird life. Its front gallery, facing down the Arima Valley, is equipped for observation as well as relaxation.

Oil is the foundation of the economy: the major reserves are off Trinidad's south-east coast, where this rig is operating.

St Stephen's Church, Princes Town. In 1880, Prince Albert and Prince George (later King George V) visited Trinidad: Princes Town, in the rolling south Trinidad countryside, was renamed in their honour, and the princes planted a Poui tree by the church.

Sugar-cane, for many decades
the lifeblood of the economy,
is still grown, mainly on the
wide plains of central and
south Trinidad.

The Pitch Lake at La Brea is a
rare example of a lake of
natural asphalt, over 250 feet
deep and self-replenishing.

Superb palm-fringed beaches
run down Trinidad's eastern,
Atlantic coast. These new
Tourist Board facilities are at
Manzanilla.

Tobago

Tobago's coast, with its reefs and cliffs, its sandy beaches and rock formations, offers some of the best diving in the world.

Fort King George, above Scarborough, was Tobago's major defensive position, its massive cannon pointing out into the sea lanes and the oncoming trade winds.

Courland Bay: some of Tobago's earliest settlers came from Latvia and made a home near this lovely curve of beach.

11

Pulling in the seine at
Courland Bay.

Buccoo Reef is the most
famous of the many reefs
fringing the Tobago coast,
offering easy access to a
fascinating underwater world.

The ferry from Trinidad ties
up near the Scarborough Mall.

The international golf course
at Mount Irvine is the scene of
many a world-class
tournament.

Visitors to Buccoo Reef can take time to swim in the warm water of the Nylon Pool on their way back.

This lovely sweep of coastline unfolds below the lookout at Speyside on the Atlantic coast.

Tobago belle.

The sun sets over Pigeon Point.

Tobago's most famous beach: Pigeon Point.

Carnival, Calypso and Pan

Most of the people of Trinidad and Tobago pour onto the streets for Carnival — to join a band, to watch, or to move along with the revellers.

Panorama is the big annual competition for steel orchestras, culminating just before Carnival.

16

The children come out in force for their own Carnival every year.

The calypsonians are the heroes of the Carnival season; among the most popular is Gypsy, crowned Calypso King of the World in 1987.

Calypsonian Black Stalin, several times Trinidad and Tobago's Calypso Monarch.

Perhaps nobody has made a bigger contribution to calypso than the most famous of them all — the Mighty Sparrow.

This Indian squaw is out to enjoy her Carnival...

Carnival costumes turn into mobile sculptures...

Every other year, the steel orchestras compete in a Steelband Music Festival, playing everything from complex classical works to calypso.

Festivals

With its rich variety of races and religions, Trinidad and Tobago is rich in festivals. Phagwah is the Hindu spring festival.

The Muslim festival of Hosay
involves the building of giant
tadjahs, like this one at
Cedros; while in the Port of
Spain suburb of St James,
musicians tune their tassa
drums for the procession.

The flickering deyas of Divali,
the Hindu festival of lights,
cover the Aranguez Savannah
near Port of Spain.

The call to prayer, during the Muslim festival of Eid-ul-Fitr, marking the end of the Ramadan fast.

Folk traditions are kept vibrantly alive by the annual Best Village Competition. Dancers perform a human limbo...
... and portray one of the major Carnival characters, the Pierrot Grenade.

Goat-racing is a tradition of
the Tobago village of Buccoo,
especially on Easter Tuesday.

The annual fishing tournament
in Tobago produces some
spectacular catches . . .

The Great Race from Trinidad
to Tobago attracts dozens of
powerboats and thousands of
festive spectators each
summer.

The Chaconia, the national flower, is named after the last and greatest Spanish governor, Chacon, and blooms around independence time in late August.

Nature

The vivid scarlet umbrella of the Flamboyant adds splashes of colour to the landscape of both islands.

The yellow and pink Poui trees burst into bloom for a few brief days during the dry season, carpeting the ground with fallen flowers.

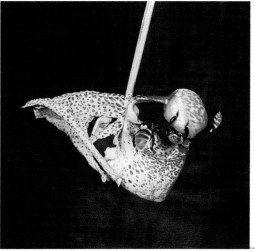

One of the most handsome ground orchids is the *Pogonia rosea*, which flowers at the start of the rainy season and grows to about 80 cm.

The Spider orchid, *Brassia caudata*, grows in the forest and reaches about 35 cm.

One of the most profuse and handsome orchids, the *Epidendrum cristatum.*

The Monkey Throat orchid, *Coryanthes macrantha*. It produces one large bee-pollinated flower.

Trinidad is the richest site in the Eastern Caribbean for orchids: its ancient connection with the South American continent and the survival of primary forest help to create an unparalleled variety of habitats.

The Scarlet Ibis is Trinidad's national bird; it roosts and sometimes nests in the mangrove swamps. One of the most spectacular sights in the country is the flocks of Scarlet Ibis returning to the Caroni Swamp in the last hour of daylight.

The Kiskadee is perhaps the best-known bird in Trinidad, distinguished by its persistent cry (kis-ka-dee, or *qu'est-ce qu'il dit?*).

The Magnificent Frigatebird, or Man-o'-War Bird, is a common sight along Trinidad and Tobago's coasts; its outstretched wings reach seven feet.

The Red Anartia is probably the most common butterfly in Trinidad and Tobago.

The '89' butterfly, named after the patterns on the underside of its wings, is a fairly small butterfly preferring higher ground.

The glorious Emperor butterfly with its large wingspan and deep iridescent blue is the only member of the Morphidae family to penetrate the Caribbean from Central and South America.

Living

Dancers are among the most exciting of Trinidad and Tobago's performing artists.

African religious tradition meshed with Christian evangelism ... a baptism ceremony gets under way.

About a quarter of the population is Hindu. This Hindu temple is in a private home near Port of Spain.

The wayside shop and café is a mainstay of communities throughout the country; this one is near Manzanilla.

The traditional clay oven is still in use in this house in the village of Matura.

Sea grapes ...

These splendid ceremonial helmets are used by the Mounted Police.

Never mind the heat: marathons, half-marathons and 10 km races are regular events. Here, runners taking part in the annual Trinidad and Tobago Marathon move through Chaguanas.

The sun sets over tranquil
Back Bay in Tobago.